GROUND BREAKERS
BLACK MUSICIANS

ARETHA FRANKLIN

by Joyce Markovics

CHERRY LAKE PRESS
Ann Arbor, Michigan

CHERRY LAKE PRESS

Published in the United States of America by Cherry Lake Publishing
Ann Arbor, Michigan
www.cherrylakepublishing.com

Reading Adviser: Beth Walker Gambro, MS, Ed., Reading Consultant, Yorkville, IL
Content Adviser: Michael Kramer, PhD, Music Historian
Book Designer: Ed Morgan

Photo Credits: © Wikimedia Commons, cover and title page; © Adam Scull/Alamy Stock Photo, 5; Wikimedia Commons/
WillyBearden, 6; © Universal Images Group North America LLC/Alamy Stock Photo, 7; © Everett Collection Inc/Alamy Stock Photo,
8; © Everett Collection Historical/Alamy Stock Photo, 9; © ZUMA Press, Inc./Alamy Stock Photo, 10; © Pictorial Press Ltd/Alamy
Stock Photo, 11; Wikimedia Commons, 12; © Granamour Weems Collection/Alamy Stock Photo, 13; © Phillipe Gras/Alamy Stock
Photo, 14; Wikimedia Commons/Moneta Sleet Jr., 15 top; Wikimedia Commons, 15 bottom; © mark reinstein/Shutterstock, 16;
© Steffano Chiacchiarini '74 /Shutterstock, 17; © MediaPunch Inc/Alamy Stock Photo, 18; © REUTERS/Alamy Stock Photo, 19;
© MediaPunch Inc/Alamy Stock Photo, 21; freepik.com, 22.

Library of Congress Cataloging-in-Publication Data

Names: Markovics, Joyce L., author.
Title: Aretha Franklin / by Joyce Markovics.
Description: Ann Arbor, Michigan : Cherry Lake Publishing, 2023. | Series:
  Groundbreakers: Black musicians | Includes bibliographical references
  and index. | Audience: Grades 4-6
Identifiers: LCCN 2023003452 (print) | LCCN 2023003453 (ebook) | ISBN
  9781668927809 (hardcover) | ISBN 9781668928851 (paperback) | ISBN
  9781668930328 (epub) | ISBN 9781668931806 (pdf) | ISBN 9781668933282
  (kindle edition) | ISBN 9781668934760 (ebook)
Subjects: LCSH: Franklin, Aretha—Juvenile literature. | Soul
  musicians—United States—Biography. | African American
  singers—Biography—Juvenile literature. | Singers—United
  States—Biography—Juvenile literature.
Classification: LCC ML3930.F68 M37 2023 (print) | LCC ML3930.F68 (ebook)
  | DDC 782.421644092 [B]—dc23/eng/20230125
LC record available at https://lccn.loc.gov/2023003452
LC ebook record available at https://lccn.loc.gov/2023003453

Printed in the United States of America by
Corporate Graphics

Note from publisher: Websites change regularly, and their future contents are outside of our control.
Supervise children when conducting any recommended online searches for extended learning opportunities.

CONTENTS

THIS IS ARETHA

Called the "Queen of Soul," Aretha Franklin helped shape American music. Using her powerful, soulful voice, she recorded dozens of hit songs. With feeling and honesty, Aretha sang what people felt. Yet she was more than a gifted singer. Aretha raised her voice to fight for **racial** equality. For her, "Respect" was more than a song. It reflected "the need of a nation, the need of the average man and woman in the street," Aretha said.

> "WE ALL REQUIRE AND WANT RESPECT, MAN OR WOMAN, BLACK OR WHITE. IT'S OUR BASIC HUMAN RIGHT."
> —ARETHA FRANKLIN

Aretha Franklin, the groundbreaking singer and songwriter

Aretha Franklin won 18 Grammy Awards and sold more than 75 million albums!

EARLY LIFE

On March 25, 1942, Aretha Louise Franklin was born in Memphis, Tennessee. Her mom, Barbara, was a skilled piano player and singer. And C.L., her dad, was a popular preacher with a "million-dollar voice." They had four children together. But their home was not always happy. "My parents' relationship was stormy," said Aretha's sister Erma.

This is the home in Memphis, Tennessee, where Aretha Franklin was born.

Aretha was called "Ree" by her family.

In 1948, Aretha's parents split up. Barbara left the family. Aretha and her siblings moved to Detroit, Michigan, with their dad. "We were all devastated," said Erma. Aretha, who was very close to her mom, cried for days.

Aretha's father was a well-known **activist**. He fought for **civil rights** alongside his friend Dr. Martin Luther King Jr.

When Aretha was only 10 years old, her heart broke again. Her mom died from a sudden heart attack. Later, Aretha wrote, "I cannot describe the pain, nor will I try." Aretha sank into **despair**. She was unable to talk for weeks. Her dad encouraged her to sing. He said, "Without the music, I'm not sure Aretha would have found her way out of the shell."

According to one of her sisters, Aretha was an excellent student who did well in all of her classes.

"I DIDN'T REALLY WANT TO SING AT FIRST, BUT MY DAD INSISTED THAT I DO."
—ARETHA FRANKLIN

Aretha started singing **gospel** music with her father. Because she was still so young, she stood on a chair to sing solos in church. "My **mentor** was Clara Ward of the famous Ward gospel singers," said Aretha. "And my dad was my coach. . . . And just my natural love for music is what drove me." Aretha's first album, *The Gospel Sound of Aretha Franklin*, was released in 1956. She was just 14 years old.

Clara Ward (center) with her gospel group, The Famous Ward Singers

As a child, Aretha learned how to play the piano by listening to the notes.

C.L. knew his daughter had a special talent. And Aretha had found her passion. "Sometimes, what you are looking for is already there," she said. Aretha joined her preacher dad and other gospel musicians on tour. At age 16, she toured with Dr. Martin Luther King Jr. as a gospel singer. By her sophomore year, she dropped out of high school.

Aretha as a young performer

In 1960, Aretha got a record deal as a pop singer. One of the singles on her album was "Today I Sing the Blues." **Critics** saw her talent. But many thought she wasn't getting the success she deserved. When she was 18 years old, Aretha married a much older man named Ted White. He treated Aretha badly. Singer and family friend Mahalia Jackson said, "I don't think she's happy. Somebody else is making her sing the **blues**."

Here's Aretha with her first husband, Ted White. The marriage ended in 1969.

Many of C.L.'s famous friends dropped by the Franklin home. They included the singers Mahalia Jackson and James Cleveland.

MAKING MUSIC

In 1966, Aretha switched record labels. A **producer** named Jerry Wexler supported her talent and style. The next year, Aretha recorded one of her most famous songs, "I Never Loved a Man (The Way I Loved You)." Fans could hear the blues and gospel roots in her voice. The song was a smash hit. Then came "Respect," a cover of an Otis Redding song. "Everyone wants respect," said Aretha. The song became an **anthem** for struggling women, especially women of color.

"Think" was released as part of the album, *Aretha Now.*

"I LIKE WRITING AND DON'T CONFINE MYSELF TO JUST THE WORDS OR JUST THE MUSIC."
—ARETHA FRANKLIN

12

One of Aretha's early album covers

In 1968, Aretha released "Think," a song she wrote with Ted. She belted out, "Think about what you're trying to do to me. . . . Let your mind go, let yourself be free." The song **resonated** with people everywhere. A radio personality crowned Aretha the "Queen of Soul."

Aretha's career was on fire. She had become the most successful singer in America by 1968. More hit songs followed. That year, she earned her first two Grammy Awards. Aretha toured the world. During one performance, excited fans strewed the stage with flower petals.

Aretha often performed with her sisters, Erma and Carolyn, who sang backup on many of her albums.

"MUSIC CHANGES, AND I'M GONNA CHANGE RIGHT ALONG WITH IT."
—ARETHA FRANKLIN

Aretha's success grew from there. She released more chart-topping songs on her album, *Lady Soul*. These included "Chain of Fools" and "I Say a Little Prayer." Another flood of top-ten singles came in the 1970s. But by 1975, Aretha's albums and songs were not selling as well. That didn't keep Aretha from making more music.

Dr. Martin Luther King Jr.'s wife, Coretta Scott King, and his young daughter at his funeral

Dr. Martin Luther King Jr.

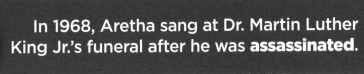

In 1968, Aretha sang at Dr. Martin Luther King Jr.'s funeral after he was **assassinated**.

In 1982, with help from singer and producer Luther Vandross, Aretha made a comeback. Her songs "Jump to It" and "Freeway of Love" were pop hits. After that, she had fewer hits. But Aretha kept performing and wowing fans. At the same time, she tried to make the world a better and fairer place for Black people.

As a performer, Aretha loved fashion and dressing up.

Aretha could even sing opera! In 1998, she sang an **aria** after opera star Luciano Pavarotti became ill.

Throughout her career, Aretha fought for social change. She held concerts to raise money for Black civil rights groups. When activist and professor Angela Davis was unjustly jailed, Aretha spoke out. "I'm going to see her free if there is any **justice** in our courts . . . she wants freedom for Black people." Aretha felt strongly that "being a **diva** is not all about singing. It has much to do with your service to people."

"I'M THE LADY NEXT DOOR WHEN I'M NOT ON STAGE."
—ARETHA FRANKLIN

During her life, Aretha received countless awards and honors. In 1987, she became the first woman **inducted** into the Rock and Roll Hall of Fame. A few years later, Aretha received a Grammy Lifetime Achievement Award. In 2005, she received one of her greatest honors, the Presidential Medal of Freedom. It's one of the top awards in the United States.

Aretha and President Barack Obama

"IN TERMS OF HELPING PEOPLE UNDERSTAND AND KNOW EACH OTHER A LITTLE BETTER, MUSIC IS UNIVERSAL."
—ARETHA FRANKLIN

She also performed for **royalty** and presidents. In 2009, Aretha sang at President Obama's **inauguration**. She wailed, "My Country, 'Tis of Thee" for the nation's first Black president. President Obama fought off tears. "American history wells up when Aretha sings," he later said.

An image from President Obama's first inauguration

Aretha was called "a musical genius unmatched in her range, power, and soul" by *National Geographic*.

ARETHA'S IMPACT

Aretha struggled with health issues, including cancer, in her later years. On August 16, 2018, she died at her home in Detroit. The nation **mourned** her loss and celebrated her five-decade career. President Obama said that she "helped define the American experience."

The Queen of Soul also inspired other Black women singers, such as Whitney Houston, Chaka Khan, and Mary J. Blige. "She is the reason why women want to sing," said Mary. As one of the most famous and gifted American singers, this groundbreaker will forever be remembered.

"I THINK IT WOULD BE A FAR GREATER WORLD IF PEOPLE WERE KINDER AND MORE RESPECTFUL TO EACH OTHER."
—ARETHA FRANKLIN

The Queen of Soul was 76 years old when she passed away.

Aretha had four sons and four grandchildren during her lifetime.

GREATEST HITS

Here are some of Aretha Franklin's signature songs:

Respect

I Say a Little Prayer

Chain of Fools

Until You Come Back to Me (That's What I'm Gonna Do)

Today I Sing the Blues

Think

Ain't No Way

I Never Loved a Man (The Way I Love You)

Do Right Woman, Do Right Man

Amazing Grace

GLOSSARY

activist (AK-tuh-vist) a person who fights for a cause

anthem (AN-them) an uplifting song identified with a group

aria (AHR-ee-uh) a long opera song

assassinated (uh-SASS-uh-nate-id) murdered

blues (BLOOZ) a type of music started by Black people in the South, often played on the guitar or the piano

civil rights (SIV-uhl RITES) the rights everyone should have to freedom and equal treatment under the law, regardless of who they are

critics (KRIT-iks) people who judge something

despair (dih-SPAIR) hopelessness

diva (DEE-vuh) a distinguished female singer

gospel (GOS-puhl) a style of religious music

inauguration (in-aw-gyuh-RAY-shuhn) a ceremony where public officials are sworn into office

inducted (in-DUHKT-uhd) brought in as a member

justice (JUHSS-tiss) fair behavior and treatment

mentor (MEN-tawr) a wise and trusted teacher

mourned (MORND) felt very sad about someone who died

producer (pruh-DOOSS-ur) the person who is in charge of making a musical recording and helping shape the overall sound

racial (RAY-shuhl) relating to the socially constructed groupings people are sometimes divided into based on the color of their skin

resonated (REZ-uh-neyt-uhd) filled with images, memories, and emotions

royalty (ROI-uhl-tee) members of a ruler's family, including kings and queens

FIND OUT MORE

BOOKS

Levy, Joel. *Turn It Up! A Pitch-Perfect History of Music That Rocked the World*. Washington, DC: National Geographic Kids, 2019.

Medina, Nico. *Who Was Aretha Franklin?* New York, NY: Penguin, 2018.

Richards, Mary, and David Schweitzer. *A History of Music for Children*. London, UK: Thames & Hudson, 2021.

WEBSITES
Explore these online sources with an adult:

Britannica Kids: Aretha Franklin

Detroit Historical Society: Aretha Franklin

Rock & Roll Hall of Fame: Aretha Franklin

INDEX

ABOUT THE AUTHOR

Joyce Markovics has written hundreds of books for kids. She appreciates the power of music to move and unite us. Joyce is grateful to all people who have beaten the odds to tell their stories and make great art. She lovingly dedicates this book to Lois.

BARACK
OBAMA

PIVOTAL PRESIDENTS
Profiles in Leadership

BARACK
OBAMA

Edited by Sherman Hollar

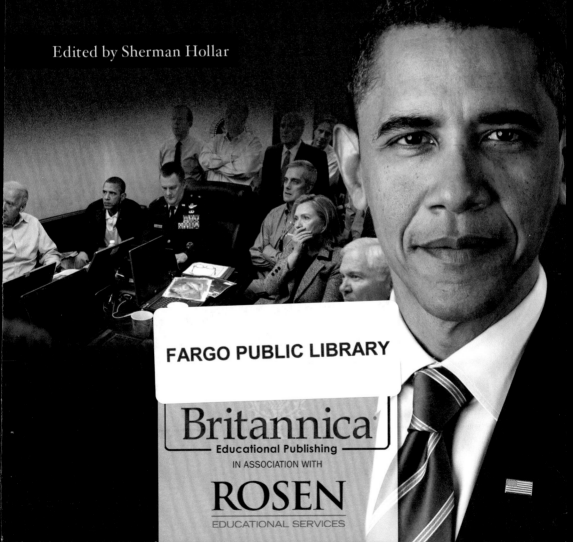

Britannica
Educational Publishing
IN ASSOCIATION WITH

ROSEN
EDUCATIONAL SERVICES

Published in 2013 by Britannica Educational Publishing
(a trademark of Encyclopædia Britannica, Inc.) in association with Rosen Educational Services, LLC
29 East 21st Street, New York, NY 10010.

Distributed exclusively by Rosen Educational Services.
For a listing of additional Britannica Educational Publishing titles, call toll free (800) 237-9932.

First Edition

Britannica Educational Publishing
J.E. Luebering: Director, Core Reference Group, Encyclopædia Britannica
Adam Augustyn: Assistant Manager, Encyclopædia Britannica

Anthony L. Green: Editor, Compton's by Britannica
Michael Anderson: Senior Editor, Compton's by Britannica
Andrea R. Field: Senior Editor, Compton's by Britannica
Sherman Hollar: Senior Editor, Compton's by Britannica

Marilyn L. Barton: Senior Coordinator, Production Control
Steven Bosco: Director, Editorial Technologies
Lisa S. Braucher: Senior Producer and Data Editor
Yvette Charboneau: Senior Copy Editor
Kathy Nakamura: Manager, Media Acquisition

Rosen Educational Services
Hope Lourie Killcoyne: Executive Editor
Nelson Sá: Art Director
Cindy Reiman: Photography Manager
Karen Huang: Photo Researcher
Brian Garvey: Designer, Cover Design
Introduction by Hope Lourie Killcoyne

Library of Congress Cataloging-in-Publication Data

Barack Obama/edited by Sherman Hollar.—1st ed.
    p. cm.—(Pivotal presidents—profiles in leadership)
"In association with Britannica Educational Publishing, Rosen Educational Services."
Includes bibliographical references and index.
ISBN 978-1-61530-945-0 (library binding)
1. Obama, Barack—Juvenile literature. 2. Presidents—United States—Biography—Juvenile literature.
I. Hollar, Sherman, ed.
E908.B337 2010
973.932092—dc23
[B]

                                                                            2012034011

Manufactured in the United States of America

On the cover, p. 3: Behind the portrait of Barack Obama, 44th president of the United States, is a
key moment from his presidency, showing Pres. Barack Obama (*seated second from left*) and various
government officials—including Vice Pres. Joe Biden (*seated left*), Secretary of Defense Robert M. Gates
(*seated right*), and Secretary of State Hillary Clinton (*seated second from right*)—receiving updates in the
Situation Room of the White House during the Osama bin Laden mission, May 2011. *The White House/
Getty Images*

Cover, p. 3 (Obama portrait) The White House; cover, pp. 1, 3 (flag) © iStockphoto.com/spxChrome;
pp. 5, 14, 25, 34, 44, 72, 74, 77, 78 *Fedorov Oleksiy/Shutterstock.com*

Table of Contents

INTRODUCTION

Following his victory speech on election night, Nov. 6, 2012, U.S. Pres. Barack Obama waves to supporters in Chicago, Ill. Chip Somodevilla/Getty Images

History, circumstance, and even nomenclature would seem to have been fairly strong bulwarks against the possibility of Barack Hussein Obama II ever becoming president of the United States of America.

History first. No black man had ever held the office. In fact, when Obama became a U.S. senator for Illinois in 2005, he was only the third African American since Reconstruction ended (in 1877) to have been elected to that body.

Circumstance. Obama was born in Hawaii. Another first for a U.S. president. (And consider that even two years after he was elected president, a CBS News poll reported that 25 percent of Americans did not believe that he was born in the United States.) What is more, Obama was born to a white (American) mother and black (Kenyan) father, the two of whom divorced when Obama was three years old. He then moved with his mother and stepfather to Indonesia, spending several years of his childhood there. Obama's upbringing was, for some Americans, all a bit foreign, alien, and undesirable.

And then there's nomenclature: his name. Barack? Not exactly from the usual pool of presidential first names. Further, his *last* name rhymes with the *first* name of the most notorious terrorist of our time: al-Qaeda leader Osama bin Laden. And as for the middle name—Hussein—well, that is also completely off the nomenclatural charts. (At an October 2012 charity event attended by both Obama and his 2012 Republican presidential rival, Willard Mitt Romney—who goes by his middle name—the president quipped wistfully: "I wish I could use *my* middle name.")

So much for external variables. What about the man and the president himself? In this book, you will learn much about Barack Obama's life during both his pre-presidential and presidential years.

As for his presidency, so much happened during his first term alone that it might be illuminating for readers to simply see a list of some of the issues, challenges, and triumphs of those years:

- Obama is awarded the Nobel Peace Prize in 2009.
- Obama declares that he will close the military prison in Guantánamo Bay, Cuba, within a year of his becoming president. He fails to do so.

- An economic crisis had emerged in 2008 during the presidency of George W. Bush, which the newly elected Obama fights with a nearly $800 billion stimulus package. The influx of money was seen as the right move by many, but not all. One positive result was that it helps take General Motors from bankruptcy in June 2009 to financial recovery by May 2010.

- The politically conservative Tea Party movement, first mobilized in opposition to Obama's moves toward health care reform, is formed in 2009. Obama himself serves as a powerful recruiting tool, as the Tea Party ranks are swelled by "Birthers"—individuals who claim that Obama was born outside of the United States and thus was not eligible to serve as president (despite the fact that his birth certificate is ultimately made available to the public)—as well as by those who consider Obama a socialist and those who believe Obama, who frequently discussed publicly his Christianity, is secretly a Muslim.

- The 2010 Deepwater Horizon oil spill in the Gulf of Mexico throws the region (and beyond) into economic and environmental turmoil. By the time the spill is brought under control in July 2010, an estimated 4.9 million barrels of oil had been released into the water. Following demands by Obama, the oil company BP creates a $20 billion compensation fund for those affected by the spill.
- America continues to be involved in wars in Iraq and Afghanistan. As promised, Obama ends one (Iraq) in 2010, and he pledges to end U.S. combat involvement in Afghanistan by 2014.
- Political gridlock in Congress, notably after the midterm elections of 2010, dramatically stalls legislative progress.
- Uncomfortably high unemployment rates and an overall slow economic recovery continue to rattle the nation.
- President Obama deals with the various forms of rising instability in the Middle East by sending messages of support to demonstrators with

democratic aspirations and involving the U.S. military (for a brief time) only in the Libyan Revolt of 2011.

- The successful raid by U.S. forces in May 2011 that results in the killing of bin Laden is viewed as showing President Obama to be a decisive, quick-thinking leader who takes action.

- The Supreme Court's June 2012 decision to uphold the Patient Protection and Affordable Care Act is seen as a huge victory for Obama as it preserves the signature legislative achievement of his administration.

- On September 11, 2012, an attack on the U.S. diplomatic post in Benghazi, Libya, results in the death of four Americans, including the U.S. ambassador to Libya. Initial statements by Obama administration officials about why the attack occurred—statements that later proved to be inaccurate—are roundly condemned by Mitt Romney and his supporters.

- In October 2012 the U.S. unemployment rate reaches its lowest point since Obama's inauguration, an encouraging sign amid a struggling economy. The protracted reelection process, which takes place in a deeply divisive political environment, takes Obama away from the Oval Office onto the campaign trail for extended periods of time in 2012.

- Superstorm Sandy, which hits the East Coast and mid-Atlantic states the last week of October, kills more than 100 Americans and inflicts much property damage as it moves north. The image of Obama and New Jersey's Republican Gov. Chris Christie—up to that point one of the president's most vocal critics— touring devastated areas in his state and bringing promises of rapid aid is a remarkable demonstration of bipartisan leadership by both men.

- And then, after the most expensive presidential campaign in U.S. history (thanks in part to the Supreme Court's 2010 decision in *Citizens United* v. *Federal Election Commission*, whereby powerful political action committees, or "super PACs," were

permitted to accept unlimited con-
tributions from sources who often
remained effectively anonymous—
not to mention the billions in
donations raised by each candidate),
the votes were tallied, and Barack
Obama won another term in office
by a comfortable margin in the electoral college and just over 50 percent
of the popular vote.

Read on for more details about Barack
Obama: from his early life to his entry into
politics to the challenges of his first term and
the challenges that await.

CHAPTER 1

Early Life

In only four years Barack Obama made an improbable rise from the state legislature of Illinois to the highest office of the United States. The first African American to win the presidency, he made history with his resounding victory in the election of 2008. His eloquent message of hope and change attracted voters across the country, even in states that had gone decades without supporting a Democratic presidential candidate.

CHILDHOOD AND FAMILY BACKGROUND

Obama's father, Barack Obama, Sr., was from rural Kenya, where he grew up herding

Barack Obama is sworn in as the 44th president of the United States on Jan. 20, 2009. MSgt Cecilio Ricardo, U.S. Air Force/U.S. Department of Defense

A young Barack Obama is seen in this undated photograph with his father, Barack Obama, Sr. AP Photo/Obama for America

goats. He won a scholarship to study in the United States and eventually became a senior economist in the Kenyan government. Obama's mother, S. Ann Dunham, grew up in Kansas, Texas, and Washington state before her family settled in Honolulu. In 1960 she and Barack Sr. met in a Russian language class at the University of Hawaii and married less than a year later. Barack Hussein Obama II was born on Aug. 4, 1961, in Honolulu.

When Barack was two years old, Barack Sr. left to study at Harvard University; shortly thereafter, in 1964, he and Ann divorced.

Left: *An undated photograph shows Barack Obama with his mother, S. Ann Dunham.* AP Photo/Obama Presidential Campaign

Right: *Barack Obama romps on the beach with his grandfather, Stanley Armour Dunham, sometime during the 1960s.* AP Photo/Obama Presidential Campaign

(Obama saw his father only one more time, during a brief visit when Obama was 10.) Later Ann remarried, this time to another foreign student, Lolo Soetoro from Indonesia, with whom she had a second child, Maya. Obama lived for several years in Jakarta with his half sister, mother, and stepfather. While there, Obama attended both a government-run school where he received some instruction in Islam and a Catholic private school where he took part in Christian schooling.

He returned to Hawaii in 1971 and lived in a modest apartment, sometimes with his grandparents and sometimes with his mother (she remained for a time in Indonesia, returned to Hawaii, and then went abroad again—partly to pursue work on a Ph.D.— before divorcing Soetoro in 1980). For a brief period his mother was aided by government food stamps, but the family mostly lived a middle-class existence.

EDUCATION AND MARRIAGE

In 1979 Obama graduated from Punahou School, an elite college preparatory academy in Honolulu. After high school he attended Occidental College in suburban Los Angeles for two years. He then transferred to Columbia University in New York City, where he received a bachelor's degree in political science in 1983. Influenced by professors who pushed him to take his studies more seriously, Obama experienced great intellectual growth during college and for a couple of years thereafter. He led a rather ascetic life and read works of literature and philosophy by William Shakespeare,

Barack Obama escorting Laura Kong during the graduation ceremony at Punahou School in May 1979, Honolulu, Hawaii. Laura S. L. Kong/Hulton Archive/Getty Images

Friedrich Nietzsche, Toni Morrison, and others. After serving as a writer and editor for Business International Corp.—a research, publishing, and consulting firm in Manhattan—he took a position in 1985 as a community organizer in Chicago. In this position he worked with churches to improve living conditions in impoverished neighborhoods on the city's South Side. He returned to school three years later and graduated magna cum laude in 1991 from

Barack Obama on the day after being elected president of the **Harvard Law Review,** *Feb. 7, 1990.* **Steve Liss/Time & Life Pictures/Getty Images**

Michelle Obama

An attorney and university administrator, Michelle Obama is also the wife of Barack Obama, the 44th president of the United States. She won many admirers by striking a firm balance between her private family life and her highly public role in her husband's political career.

Michelle LaVaughn Robinson was born on Jan. 17, 1964, in Chicago and grew up on the city's South Side. She studied sociology and African American studies at Princeton University, earning a bachelor's degree in 1985. Three years later she received a degree from Harvard Law School.

Returning to Chicago after graduation, Michelle took a job as a junior associate at the law firm Sidley Austin, where she specialized in intellectual property law. Seeking a career path based in

Michelle Obama. Joyce N. Boghosian/ The White House

public service, in 1991 she became an assistant to Chicago Mayor Richard M. Daley. The following year she married Barack, who was then a community organizer. From 1992 to 1993 Michelle was the assistant commissioner for the Chicago Department of Planning and Development. In 1993 she founded the Chicago branch of Public Allies, a leadership-training program for young adults; for three years she served as the branch's executive director.

First ladies often take up various causes to promote, and for Michelle Obama one of those is the quest to promote healthy eating, especially for children. Here she is seen at a June 2012 book signing in Washington, D.C., for her book American Grown: The Story of the White House Kitchen Garden and Gardens Across America. *The book details the first lady's experiences creating what may well be America's most well-known vegetable garden.* Mark Wilson/Getty Images

In 1996 Michelle became the associate dean of student services at the University of Chicago. In that post she helped organize the school's community outreach programs. In 2002 she became the executive director of community and external affairs for the university. Three years later she became vice president of community and external affairs for the University of Chicago Medical Center.

When her husband announced his candidacy for the 2008 Democratic presidential nomination, Michelle took a prominent role in his campaign. She took leave from her position at the University of Chicago to devote herself more fully to campaigning while still maintaining time to care for her and Barack's two young daughters. An adept speaker, she stumped extensively for her husband during the long Democratic primary race and then in his general-election campaign against Republican John McCain. Michelle's openness on the campaign trail and in interviews — she often humanized her husband by discussing his faults — endeared her to many. Campaign aides referred to her as "the closer" for her persuasiveness in winning over uncommitted voters who attended rallies. Her efforts contributed to Barack's historic election to the presidency in November 2008.

Harvard University's law school, where he was the first African American to serve as president of the *Harvard Law Review*.

While working as a summer associate in 1989 at the Chicago law firm of Sidley

Barack and Michelle Obama with their daughters, Sasha (in white dress) and Malia, in the Green Room of the White House, Washington, D.C., 2009. Photo by Annie Leibovitz/Official White House Photo

Austin, Obama met Chicago native Michelle Robinson, a young lawyer at the firm. The two married in 1992 and had two daughters, Malia and Sasha.

Barack Obama Timeline

	Obama becomes a community organizer in Chicago.		Obama is elected to the Illinois Senate.		Obama is elected to the U.S. Senate.		Obama signs major health care reform legislation.
1961	1985	1991	1996	July 2004	November 2004	2008	2010
Obama is born in Honolulu, Hawaii.		Obama graduates from Harvard Law School.		Obama delivers the keynote address at the Democratic National Convention.		Obama is elected president.	

Key events in the life and first term of Barack Obama. Encyclopædia Britannica, Inc.

CHAPTER 2

Entry into Politics

O bama's rapid ascent to national political prominence began in his adopted hometown of Chicago, where he experienced early success as a candidate for elective office and laid the groundwork for future campaigns. By the time of his election to the U.S. Senate in 2004, he had become one of the most talked-about young politicians in a generation.

RETURN TO CHICAGO AND EARLY POLITICAL INVOLVEMENT

After law school Obama returned to Chicago and became active in the Democratic Party.

BARACK OBAMA

Dreams from My Father
A STORY OF RACE AND INHERITANCE

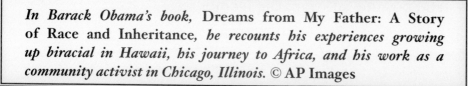

In Barack Obama's book, Dreams from My Father: A Story of Race and Inheritance, *he recounts his experiences growing up biracial in Hawaii, his journey to Africa, and his work as a community activist in Chicago, Illinois.* © AP Images

He organized Project Vote, a drive that registered tens of thousands of African Americans to vote and that was credited with helping Democrat Bill Clinton win Illinois and capture the presidency in 1992. The effort also helped make Carol Moseley Braun, an Illinois state legislator, the first African American woman elected to the U.S. Senate. During this period, Obama wrote his first book and saw it published. The memoir, *Dreams from My Father*, was released in 1995 to little fanfare, although it received generally positive reviews. The book traced Obama's personal challenge of coming to terms with his biracial heritage and described a journey he made to his father's village in Africa. (The elder Obama had died in an auto accident in 1982.) Obama also lectured on constitutional law at the University of Chicago and worked as an attorney on civil rights issues.

ELECTION TO THE STATE LEGISLATURE AND U.S. SENATE

In 1996 Obama was elected as a Democrat to the Illinois Senate, where he would serve

for eight years. As a state senator he helped pass legislation that tightened campaign finance regulations, expanded health care to poor families, and reformed criminal justice and welfare laws. He also served as chairman of the state's Health and Human Services Committee.

In 2004 Obama ran for a seat in the U.S. Senate. In the Democratic primary he emerged as the winner from a field of seven candidates. During the general election campaign Obama's Republican opponent was forced to withdraw after damaging details of his divorce proceedings came to light. The state Republican Party then brought in Alan Keyes, a conservative radio talk-show host and former diplomat who moved to Illinois from Maryland for the contest. It was the first Senate race in which the two leading candidates were African Americans. Obama handily defeated Keyes in November,

A 1999 file photo of then-Illinois State Senator Barack Obama.
Chicago Tribune/McClatchy-Tribune/Getty Images

winning 70 percent of the vote. He was only the third African American to be elected to the Senate since the end of Reconstruction in 1877.

RISE OF A POLITICAL SUPERSTAR

It was while campaigning for the U.S. Senate that Obama first gained national

U.S. Senate candidate Barack Obama the night before he made his now-famous speech at the 2004 Democratic National Convention, Boston, Mass. Chris Maddaloni/CQ-Roll Call Group/Getty Images

recognition. He was chosen to deliver the keynote address at the Democratic National Convention in July 2004, and his rousing speech brought convention-eers to their feet and instantly made him a political superstar. The speech wove elements of Obama's biography with the theme that all Americans are connected in ways that transcend political, cultural, and geographical differences. Following the address, Obama's memoir climbed the best-seller lists.

After taking office as a senator in 2005, Obama quickly became a major figure in his party. He received several coveted committee assignments, including a post on the Foreign Relations Committee. He also served on the Environment and Public Works and the Veteran's Affairs committees. He supported ethics reform in government, championed alternative energy sources, and worked to secure or destroy deadly weapons in Russia and elsewhere.

Obama achieved a level of visibility that was rare for a first-term senator. A trip to his father's home in Kenya in August 2006 attracted international media attention.

Keynote Address at the 2004 Democratic National Convention

By the time of the 2004 election campaign, political pundits routinely divided the United States into red and blue states, whose color not only indicated which political party was locally dominant but also signified the supposed prevalence of a set of social and cultural values. According to the received wisdom, the Republican red states—generally located in the South, West, and lower Midwest—were conservative, God-fearing, pro-life on

Barack Obama delivering the keynote speech on the second day of the Democratic National Convention in Boston, July 27, 2004. Spencer Platt/Getty Images

the issue of abortion, opposed to big government and same-sex marriage, and predominantly small-town and suburban. The Democratic blue states—found mostly on the coasts, in the Northeast, and in the Upper Midwest—were liberal, secular, politically correct, pro-choice on abortion, and predominantly urban. The keynote address at the Democratic Convention in Boston was delivered by Barack Obama, who became an instant national figure with his eloquent address, in which he debunked the country's artificial red-blue division and offered "the audacity of hope," a phrase that would become the title of the book he published shortly before becoming a candidate for the 2008 presidential election. During the climactic part of his address, Obama declared:

> *Yet even as we speak, there are those who are preparing to divide us, the spin masters, the negative ad peddlers who embrace the politics of anything goes. Well, I say to them tonight, there is not a liberal America and a conservative America—there is the United States of America. There is not a black America and a white America and Latino America and Asian America; there's the United States of America. The pundits like to slice-and-dice our country into Red States and Blue States; Red States for Republicans, Blue States for Democrats. But I've got news for them, too. We worship an awesome God in the Blue States, and we don't like federal agents poking around in our libraries in the Red States. We coach Little League in the Blue States and have gay friends in the Red States. There are patriots who opposed the war in Iraq and there are patriots who supported it. We are one people, all of us pledging allegiance to the stars and stripes, all of us defending the United States of America.*

Then-U.S. Senator Barack Obama signing a copy of his book The Audacity of Hope *at a Skokie, Ill., bookstore, Oct. 18, 2006.* Tim Boyle/Getty Images

His second book, *The Audacity of Hope*, a mainstream polemic on his vision for the United States, was published weeks later and instantly became a best seller.

CHAPTER 3

Nomination and Election

In early 2007 Obama declared himself in the running for the 2008 Democratic presidential nomination. The overwhelming favorite to win the nomination was Sen. Hillary Clinton of New York. However, Obama's personal charisma, stirring oratory, and campaign promise to bring change to the political system won him the support of many Democrats, especially young and minority voters.

THE PRIMARY CAMPAIGN OF 2008

On Jan. 3, 2008, Obama won a surprise victory in the first major nominating contest, the Iowa caucus. Five days later,

WHO'S NEXT *in* 2007

SPECIAL DOUBLE ISSUE

Newsweek.

The Race *is* On

OBAMA & HILLARY
ARE ALREADY SQUARING
OFF OVER 2008. BUT IS
AMERICA READY FOR
EITHER ONE?

Barack Obama and Hillary Clinton on the cover of Newsweek,
Dec. 25, 2006–Jan. 1, 2007. PRNewsFoto/Newsweek/AP Images

however, Clinton topped Obama in the New Hampshire primary, and a bruising—and sometimes bitter—primary race ensued. Obama won more than a dozen states—including Illinois, his home state, and Missouri, a traditional political bellwether—on Super Tuesday, February 5. No clear front-runner for the nomination emerged, however, as Clinton won many states with large populations, such as California and New York. Obama produced an impressive string of victories later in the month, handily winning the 11 primaries and caucuses that immediately followed Super Tuesday, which gave him a significant lead in pledged delegates. His momentum slowed in early March when Clinton won significant victories in Ohio and Texas. Though still maintaining his edge in delegates, Obama lost the key Pennsylvania primary on April 22. Two weeks later he lost a close contest in Indiana but won the North Carolina primary by a large margin, widening his delegate lead over Clinton. She initially had a big lead in so-called superdelegates (Democratic Party officials allocated votes at the convention that were unaffiliated with state primary results), but, with Obama winning more states and actual delegates, many peeled away from her and went to Obama.

Not until June 3, following the final primaries in Montana and South Dakota, did the number of delegates pledged to Obama surpass the total needed to win the Democratic nomination. Obama officially accepted the nomination at the Democratic National Convention in August, becoming the first African American to be nominated for the presidency by either major party.

Showdown with McCain

Obama's Republican opponent for the presidency was Sen. John McCain of Arizona. When McCain criticized Obama as being too inexperienced for the office, Obama countered by choosing Joe Biden, a longtime senator from Delaware, as his vice-presidential running mate. Obama and McCain waged a fierce and expensive contest. Obama, still bolstered by a fever of popular support, eschewed federal financing of his campaign and raised hundreds of millions of dollars, much of it coming in small donations and over the Internet from a record number

OBAMA'08

YES WE CAN

WWW.**BARACKOBAMA**.COM

Memorabilia from Barack Obama's first presidential campaign.
Obama for America

of donors. Obama's fund-raising advantage helped him buy massive amounts of television advertising and organize deep grassroots organizations in key battleground states and in states that had voted Republican in previous presidential cycles.

A key issue in the hard-fought campaign was the Iraq War, with Obama calling for a swift withdrawal of most U.S. forces from Iraq while McCain insisted that the United States must wait for full victory before withdrawing. Other topics of debate were health care and taxation.

In the weeks leading up to the election, the recent collapse of some of the largest U.S. banks and financial institutions made the economy the single most important issue. The economic meltdown propelled Obama's campaign, which called the crisis a result of the policies of outgoing Republican president George W. Bush. Many voters linked McCain with the unpopular Bush, and polls indicated that the majority believed Obama was better equipped to turn the economy around.

In November 2008 Obama decisively won the presidency, capturing 365 electoral votes and some 53 percent of the

Results of the American presidential election, 2008.

popular vote. He won all the states that the Democrat John Kerry had won in the 2004 election and also captured a number of states (including Colorado, Florida, Nevada, Ohio, and Virginia) that the Republicans had carried in the previous two presidential elections. On election night tens of thousands gathered in Chicago's Grant Park to see Obama claim victory. In addition to being the first African American president,

Joe Biden

Democratic politician Joe Biden became one of the youngest senators in U.S. history when he took office in 1973. After winning reelection five times, he secured the honor of being Delaware's longest-serving senator. In 2008 he was elected vice president of the United States as the running mate of Barack Obama.

Joseph Robinette Biden, Jr., was born on Nov. 20, 1942, in Scranton, Pa. He received a bachelor's degree from the University of Delaware in 1965 followed by a law degree from Syracuse University in New York in 1968. He then worked as an attorney in Delaware, with his first venture into politics as a councilman for New Castle County from 1970 to 1972. Biden was elected to the U.S.

Joe Biden. U.S. Senator Joe Biden

Senate in 1972. In this capacity he served on the Senate's Foreign Relations Committee, becoming its chairman from 2001 to 2003 and from 2007. He also was on the Committee on the Judiciary, serving as its chair from 1987 to 1995.

Biden pursued the 1988 Democratic presidential nomination but withdrew after it was revealed that parts of his campaign stump speech had been plagiarized from British Labour Party leader Neil Kinnock. His 2008 presidential campaign never gained momentum, and he withdrew from the race in January of that year. After Obama secured the Democratic presidential nomination, he announced his selection of Biden as the Democratic Party's vice-presidential nominee in August. In November Obama and Biden defeated John McCain and his running mate, Sarah Palin. Biden resigned from the Senate shortly before taking office as vice president in January 2009.

Michelle and Barack Obama and Jill and Joe Biden at Invesco Field on the final night of the Democratic National Convention in Denver, Aug. 28, 2008. Carol M. Highsmith/Library of Congress, Washington, D.C.

Biden had a reputation for speaking candidly, and there were instances when his remarks created problems for Obama. During the 2008 campaign, Biden made headlines with his statement that if Obama were elected, he would be tested with an "international crisis" within six months of taking office—an assertion that Obama dismissed as an example of Biden's tendency toward "rhetorical flourishes." In May 2012 Biden prompted much commentary again when he expressed strong support for same-sex marriage, though Obama, as president, had not publicly made such an endorsement. Just days after Biden's comments on the issue, however, Obama stated during an interview, "At a certain point I've just concluded that for me personally, it is important for me to go ahead and affirm that I think same-sex couples should be able to get married."

At other times, Biden's candor and directness proved politically helpful to the president. That was the case during the 2012 reelection campaign, when—following what was generally perceived as a lackluster performance by Obama in the first presidential debate—Biden reenergized Democratic supporters by forcefully defending the administration's record during his vice presidential debate with Congressman Paul Ryan of Wisconsin. Both in the debate and on the campaign trail, Biden also delivered sharply worded critiques of proposals put forward by Ryan and the Republican presidential nominee, Mitt Romney.

he was also the first sitting U.S. senator to win the office since John F. Kennedy in 1960. Shortly after his win, Obama resigned from the Senate. He was inaugurated as president on Jan. 20, 2009.

CHAPTER 4

Presidency

From its outset, Obama's presidential campaign had been based on the theme of sweeping political change. He entered the White House vowing to improve the image of the United States abroad and to bring an end to partisan squabbling and legislative gridlock at home. Top domestic priorities for the new president included dealing with the economic crisis and securing the passage of far-reaching health care reforms. Key foreign-policy challenges were the ongoing wars in Iraq and Afghanistan.

ECONOMIC CHALLENGES

Responding to the economic crisis that had emerged in 2008 and prompted a rescue of the financial industry with up to $700 billion in government funds, Obama pushed through

The 2009 Nobel Peace Prize

In his first months in office, Obama worked to restore the international image of the United States, which many believed had been tarnished by the policies of the Bush administration. Obama signed an executive order that banned excessive interrogation techniques and ordered the closing of the controversial military detention facility in Guantánamo Bay, Cuba, within a year (a deadline that was not met). He vowed to work toward the elimination of nuclear weapons and to improve strained relations with Russia. In June 2009 he traveled to the Middle East and gave a speech calling for a new relationship between the United States and the Muslim world. In recognition of such efforts, Obama was awarded the 2009 Nobel Peace Prize, with the Nobel committee citing his "extraordinary efforts to strengthen international diplomacy and cooperation between peoples."

Chairman of the Norwegian Nobel Committee Thorbøjrn Jagland looks on as Pres. Barack Obama stands with his diploma and gold medal during the Nobel ceremony in Oslo, Norway, Dec. 10, 2009. Jan Johannessen/Getty Images

Congress a $787 billion stimulus package. By the third quarter of 2009 the plan had succeeded in reversing a steep decline in gross domestic product (GDP), though unemployment had also risen. Moreover, Republicans complained that the stimulus package cost too much, having swelled the federal deficit to $1.42 trillion. Still, it appeared that the U.S. economy was recovering, though slowly. The president could proudly point to the dramatic turnaround of General Motors: in June 2009 GM had lapsed into bankruptcy, necessitating a $60 billion government rescue and

Pres. Barack Obama meeting with members of his cabinet in the Cabinet Room at the White House, 2009. **Photograph by Pete Souza/ The White House**

takeover of about three-fifths of its stock, but by May 2010 the auto manufacturer, employing a new business plan, had shown its first profit in three years.

Although Obama had pledged to reduce partisanship in Washington, he made little progress in that direction in his first year. Indeed, the $787 billion stimulus package had been passed in the House of Representatives without a single Republican vote. With Democrats holding substantial majorities in both houses, Obama allowed congressional leaders to shape important legislation, and

Pres. Barack Obama talks to an appreciative crowd at the General Motors auto plant in Hamtramck, Mich., July 30, 2010. Jim Watson/AFP/ Getty Images

Republicans, claiming that they were being
largely excluded from substantive negotia-
tions on key bills, took what most Democrats
saw as an obstructionist approach, earning
the nickname the "Party of No" from liberal
commentators. In early 2010 Obama looked
forward to "Recovery Summer," anticipating
the payoff of the massive federal investment in
infrastructure-improvement programs aimed
at creating jobs and stimulating the economy.
But as the summer of 2010 progressed, the
prospects for the economy seemed to dim as
unemployment remained high. Some econo-
mists feared that a second recessionary period
was approaching, while others argued that the
stimulus package had been insufficient.

Obama was able to claim another major
legislative victory, however, in July, when
Congress passed (60–39 in the Senate and
237–192 in the House) a sweeping financial
reform bill. Aimed at preventing the conditions that led to the economic crisis, the
bill established a new consumer-protection
bureau, empowered the government to take
over and shut down large troubled financial
firms, and created a council of federal regula-
tors to monitor the financial system, among
other provisions.

Following the 2010 midterm elections, in
which the Democrats fared poorly, the new

Republican majority in the House locked horns with the still Democratic-controlled Senate and the Obama administration over the federal budget for fiscal year 2011. Unable to agree on that budget, the previous Congress, in October 2010, had passed the first in a series of stopgap measures to keep the federal government operating until agreement could be reached on a long-term budget. Both Republicans and Democrats believed that reductions to the budget were necessary in response to the federal government's soaring deficit; however, they disagreed vehemently on the extent, targets, and timing of budget cuts. House Republicans upped the political ante when they announced that they would not vote for another temporary budget and demanded deep reductions. The threat of a shutdown of all but essential services of the federal government came within a few hours of being realized, but on April 8, 2011, an agreement was reached that resulted in passage a week later by both the House (260–167) and the Senate (81–19) of a compromise budget for the remainder of the fiscal year that cut $38 billion in federal spending.

The following month government borrowing reached the congressionally mandated national debt ceiling of $14.29 trillion, but, by shifting funds, the Treasury Department was able to forestall the anticipated deadline for default on the public debt until August 2. Just two days before the new deadline, an agreement was reached by Obama and congressional leaders of both parties whereby the ceiling would be raised in two main stages by some $2.4 trillion, with equivalent cuts to the deficit to be achieved over a 10-year period. A final bill to increase the debt limit was passed by the House by a vote of 269–161 and by the Senate by a vote of 74–26. Yet despite these efforts, on August 5 Standard & Poor's, one of the three principal companies that advise investors on debt securities, downgraded the credit rating of the United States from the top level, AAA, to the next level, AA+.

HEALTH CARE REFORM

Another early priority of Obama's presidency was reforming the country's health care system. During the election campaign, Obama had called for reforms that would make health care insurance more affordable and extend coverage to tens of millions of Americans who lacked it. The issue provoked a prolonged and sometimes bitter debate, with Republicans complaining that Democratic proposals constituted a costly "government takeover" of health care. A new conservative populist movement, the Tea Party, loudly objected to the proposed health care reforms in a series of town hall meetings in summer 2009. More generally, Tea Party members opposed what they saw as excessive taxes and government involvement in the private sector.

In late 2009 the House of Representatives and Senate each passed a version of the health care bill. As congressional leaders prepared to negotiate a compromise between the two versions, the triumph of a Republican in a

Health care reform protestors during a demonstration organized by the American Grass Roots Coalition and the Tea Party Express in Washington, D.C., March 16, 2010. Jewel Samad/AFP/Getty Images

special election held to fill the Senate seat vacated by Ted Kennedy's death destroyed the Democrats' filibuster-proof majority. In March 2010, as the historic measure teetered on the brink of defeat, Obama and other Democratic leaders mounted a last-ditch campaign to pass it. The president became more forceful in promoting the bill, both to Congress and to the American people. Later that month Congress passed the bill with no Republican support.

The legislation—known as the Patient Protection and Affordable Care Act (PPACA)—would, once all of its elements had taken effect, prohibit denial of insurance coverage on the basis of preexisting medical conditions. It would also extend health care to some 30 million previously uninsured Americans. The bill made the attainment of health care insurance mandatory for most citizens—a requirement that was known as the individual mandate—but it also called for a tax increase on the wealthiest Americans that would largely bankroll subsidies for premium payments for families earning less than $88,000 per year. Moreover, the bill promised a tax credit to small businesses that provide coverage for their employees.

In the aftermath of the bill's passage, Republicans vowed to either repeal or replace

Pres. Barack Obama and Vice Pres. Joe Biden reacting after the U.S. House of Representatives passed the Patient Protection and Affordable Care Act, March 21, 2010. Official White House Photo by Pete Souza

the legislation, and the attorneys general in more than two dozen states filed suit, charging that the reform, in particular the individual mandate, was unconstitutional. Although a number of lawsuits were dismissed, beginning in late 2010 some federal judges agreed with the attorneys general that Congress had, by enacting the individual mandate (which was due to take effect in 2014), exceeded the authority granted it by the commerce clause of the U.S. Constitution. This clause is the legal foundation of much of the U.S. government's regulatory authority. None of these judges, however, halted the implementation of the law while the Obama administration appealed.

In March 2012 the U.S. Supreme Court heard challenges to the PPACA. Among the specific questions the Court had to resolve were determining whether the individual mandate violated the Constitution and, if so, whether the mandate was "severable" from the rest of the act's provisions (i.e., whether the other provisions would be valid if the mandate were struck down). In addition, the Court had to decide whether the act's expansion of Medicaid, the federal-state program of health insurance for the poor, amounted to an unconstitutional "coercion" of the states by the federal government.

In a 5–4 ruling issued on June 28 the Supreme Court upheld virtually all of the health care law's provisions. On the question of the individual mandate, it ruled that the provision was valid as part of the federal government's taxation powers. "The Affordable Care Act's requirement that certain individuals pay a financial penalty for not obtaining health insurance may reasonably be characterized as a tax. Because the Constitution permits such a tax, it is not our role to forbid it," the Court stated in its majority opinion, written by Chief Justice John Roberts. The Court also accepted the expansion of Medicaid, though it specified that Congress could not penalize states that choose not to participate in the expanded program. In a televised address delivered soon after the landmark ruling was announced, President Obama praised the Supreme Court's decision, calling it "a victory for people all over this country whose lives will be more secure because of this law."

FOREIGN-POLICY CHALLENGES

Throughout his presidential campaign Obama had argued that the focus of U.S. military efforts should be in Afghanistan rather than Iraq, and in keeping with this philosophy, he set an 18-month timetable for the withdrawal of U.S. combat troops from Iraq. The situation in Iraq continued to improve, and in August 2010, on schedule, the U.S. combat mission in Iraq ended. Some 50,000 U.S. troops remained in the country as a transitional force.

Meanwhile, in response to the resurgence of the Taliban (an ultraconservative political and religious faction) in Afghanistan, in February 2009 Obama raised the total U.S. troop commitment there to 68,000 and began three months of deliberations on the

U.S. Army soldiers from Charlie Company, 1st Battalion of the 3rd Infantry Regiment, disembarking from a plane at Andrews Air Force Base, Maryland, Aug. 28, 2010. The soldiers were returning from a 12-month deployment in Iraq. Nicholas Kamm/AFP/Getty Images

military's request for another 40,000 troops. He ultimately chose to deploy an additional 30,000 troops in Afghanistan, a decision that was criticized by many in his party.

In June 2010, as the Afghanistan War rivaled the Vietnam War as the longest in U.S. history and as American war deaths there topped the 1,000 mark, the president was faced with another challenge when Gen. Stanley McChrystal, commander of North Atlantic Treaty Organization (NATO)-U.S. forces in Afghanistan, and members of his staff made derisive comments about top Obama administration officials to a reporter from *Rolling Stone* magazine. Obama relieved McChrystal of command, replacing him with Gen. David Petraeus, who had been responsible for an earlier surge strategy in Iraq.

In addition to the wars in Iraq and Afghanistan, American foreign policy under Obama was tested by huge changes that took place in other parts of the Middle East. Beginning in early 2011, popular political uprisings resulted in abrupt ends to longtime authoritarian regimes in Tunisia and Egypt, and mass demonstrations took place in numerous other countries in the region. The Obama administration carefully articulated its support for the demonstrators' democratic aspirations, balancing past commitments to

U.S. Pres. Barack Obama and Stanley McChrystal, 2009. **Official White House photo by Pete Souza**

some of the threatened regimes with the U.S. advocacy of free representative government. Moreover, Obama attempted to take a role in world leadership without direct intervention in the affairs of other countries.

In Libya, however, the political revolt against the four-decade rule of Muammar al-Qaddafi turned into a civil war, and Obama felt U.S. intervention was necessary to prevent a humanitarian disaster as Qaddafi employed his overwhelming military advantage in a brutal attempt to destroy the opposition. On March 19, U.S. and European forces with warplanes and cruise missiles began attacking targets in Libya in an effort to disable Libya's air force and air defense

As part of the operation known as Odyssey Dawn, the intent of which was to prevent attacks by Libyan regime forces against its own people, the USS Barry *launches a Tomahawk missile along Libya's Mediterranean coast, March 19, 2011.* U.S. Navy/Getty Images

systems. After initially taking a leading role in these operations, the Obama administration relinquished command to NATO on March 27. Continued air strikes inflicted significant damage on pro-Qaddafi forces, and Qaddafi's hold on power was finally broken in August as rebels entered the Libyan capital, Tripoli, and took control of the city. Qaddafi was eventually killed by rebel forces in October.

This official White House photograph shows Pres. Barack Obama editing his remarks in the Oval Office prior to making a televised statement in which he announced that U.S. forces had killed Osama bin Laden. **AFP/Getty Images**

On May 1, 2011, the president made a dramatic late-night Sunday television address to inform the world that U.S. special forces had killed al-Qaeda leader Osama bin Laden in a firefight in a compound in Abbottabad, Pakistan, not far from the Pakistani capital of Islamabad. A year later, Obama traveled to Afghanistan to mark the first anniversary of bin Laden's death. While there, he and Afghan Pres. Hamid Karzai announced the signing of a strategic partnership agreement, which pledged long-term U.S. support for Afghanistan after the scheduled withdrawal of international combat forces from that country by the end of 2014.

The Hunt for Osama bin Laden

In the aftermath of the Sept. 11, 2001, terrorist attacks, U.S. Pres. George W. Bush announced that he wanted the mastermind of the attacks, Osama bin Laden, captured— dead or alive—and a $25 million bounty was eventually issued for information leading to the killing or capture of the al-Qaeda leader. Bin Laden evaded capture, however, including in December 2001, when he was tracked by U.S. forces to the mountains of Tora Bora in eastern Afghanistan. Bin Laden's trail subsequently went cold, and he was thought to be living somewhere in the Afghanistan-Pakistan tribal regions.

The Washington Post

Mostly cloudy 72/62 • Tomorrow: Thunderstorm 82/56 • **DETAILS, B6**   MONDAY, MAY 2, 2011   MD DC VA M2 V1 V2 V3 V4   *washingtonpost.com* • 75¢

'JUSTICE HAS BEEN DONE'

U.S. forces kill Osama bin Laden

PRIVILEGED SON BECAME THE GLOBAL FACE OF TERRORISM

BY BRADLEY GRAHAM

Osama bin Laden, 54, who was born into Saudi riches, only to end up leading a self-declared holy war against the United States as head of one of the most ruthless, far-flung terrorist networks in history, died Sunday in the manner he had often predicted: in a strike by U.S. forces.

As the founder of al-Qaeda, bin Laden demonstrated the power and global reach of a terrorism campaign rooted in centuries-old Islamic beliefs and skilled in modern-day technologies. The militants he inspired have proved surprisingly resilient, and the organization he established continues to pose a substantial threat to U.S. interests overseas and at home.

Although bin Laden was able

GETTY IMAGES

PUBLIC ENEMY: Bin Laden was also wanted in al-Qaeda's bombings of U.S. embassies in Tanzania and Kenya in 1998.

REUTERS

HISTORIC: Bin Laden's death will provide a clear moment of victory for Obama at a time of deep political turmoil overseas.

TEAM ATTACKED COMPOUND IN PAKISTAN WHERE HE WAS HIDING

BY SCOTT WILSON AND CRAIG WHITLOCK

Osama bin Laden has been killed in a U.S. operation in Pakistan, President Obama announced from the White House on Sunday, calling his death "the most significant achievement to date in our nation's effort to defeat al-Qaeda."

Speaking from the East Room, Obama said a small team of U.S. personnel attacked a compound Sunday in the city of Abbottabad, where bin Laden had been hiding since late last summer. After a firefight, the president said, the U.S. team killed bin Laden and "took custody of his body."

"We will be relentless in defense of our citizens and our friends and allies," a somber Obama said in his nine-minute statement "We will

The front page of The Washington Post, *May 2, 2011, the day after al-Qaeda leader Osama bin Laden was killed by U.S. forces in Pakistan, ending a nearly 10-year worldwide hunt for the mastermind of the Sept. 11 attacks.* The Washington Post/Getty Images

    U.S. intelligence eventually located him in Pakistan, living within a walled compound in the city of Abbottabad. In the early morning hours of May 2, 2011, on orders from U.S. Pres. Barack Obama, a small team of U.S. Navy SEALs invaded the compound and killed bin Laden. The SEALs used two helicopters to storm the residence — located only about 800 yards from the Pakistani army's chief officer-training academy — and shot bin Laden when he allegedly went for a weapon. His body, identified visually at the site of the raid, was taken out of Pakistan by U.S. forces for examination and DNA identification and soon after was buried at sea.

Hours after its confirmation, bin Laden's death was announced by President Obama in a televised address. "Justice has been done," the president said. "Americans understand the costs of war. Yet as a country, we will never tolerate our security being threatened, nor stand idly by when our people have been killed. We will be relentless in defense of our citizens and our friends and allies." Several days after Obama's announcement, al-Qaeda released a statement publicly acknowledging bin Laden's death and vowing revenge.

Other foreign-policy challenges emerged, including new concerns about Libya's stability. On September 11, 2012, four Americans, including the U.S. ambassador to Libya, J. Christopher Stevens, were killed in an attack on the U.S. consulate in the northeastern city of Benghazi. On the day after the attack, President Obama declared, "No acts of terror will ever shake the resolve of this great nation," and vowed "to see that justice is done for this terrible act." Although initial intelligence reports led administration officials in the following days to characterize the attack as having begun spontaneously in the wake of protests in Libya and in neighboring Egypt over an anti-Islam film made in the United States, officials later concluded it to be "a deliberate and organized terrorist attack carried out by extremists." In a speech to the United Nations General Assembly on September 25, Obama focused attention on the recent unrest in the Middle East, condemning extremism and urging world leaders to do more to prevent outbreaks of violence. He also addressed growing concerns over Iran's continuing development of its nuclear capabilities, declaring that the Iranian government had failed to show that its nuclear activities were peaceful and that the time to resolve the issue through diplomacy was "not unlimited."

CAMPAIGN FOR REELECTION

Although he effectively had been campaigning for weeks, Obama officially kicked off his reelection bid with speeches in Ohio and Virginia on May 5, 2012. The president's reelection bid was expected to be closely contested as the United States faced a number of challenges, most notably a struggling economy. Indicators showed that the economy was continuing to recover, but progress had come slowly and unevenly. Profits were up again for many corporations, big banks had returned to solid footing, and the stock market had bounced back from the dark days of the financial meltdown of 2008. Nevertheless, wages remained largely stagnant, foreclosures were still commonplace as the housing market continued its struggle to regain its balance, and unemployment figures—though improving—remained a major concern. In September 2012 the U.S. unemployment rate dropped to 7.8 percent, falling below 8 percent for the first time since February 2009.

While the Republican presidential nominee, Mitt Romney, a former governor of Massachusetts, focused much of his campaign on a critique of Obama's stewardship of the economy, Obama defended his economic record, arguing that his actions in response to the meltdown had prevented a full-scale depression and laid the foundation for recovery. "The truth is, it will take more than a few years for us to solve challenges that have built up over the decades," the president stated in his speech at the 2012 Democratic National Convention (DNC), during which he asked voters for patience with the process of completing the recovery. Whereas Romney advocated broad tax cuts and an easing of government regulations on business activity as ways to bolster economic growth, Obama called for ending tax breaks for high-income individuals (while extending them for middle- and low-income earners) and making strategic investments in such areas as transportation infrastructure, education, and clean energy.

Aside from the economy, which occupied the center stage of the campaign, the two candidates also differed on foreign policy. Obama presented his record—most notably, the withdrawal of U.S. combat troops from Iraq and his order of the daring raid that killed Osama bin Laden—as proof of his success as commander in chief. Meanwhile, Romney argued that the United States had lost momentum in world affairs under Obama's watch.

In most national polls following the DNC in September, Obama maintained a lead of at least several percentage points over Romney. In early October, however, that lead deteriorated in the wake of the first presidential debate, widely viewed to have been won by Romney. The governor's supporters sensed a turning point in the race, though experienced observers cautioned that debates had only rarely affected the outcome of presidential elections. Obama regained his stride with strong performances in the two debates that

In the wake of Hurricane Sandy, U.S. Pres. Barack Obama is greeted by New Jersey Gov. Chris Christie upon Obama's arrival in Atlantic City on October 31, 2012. The two then visited areas in New Jersey hardest hit by the high winds and rising tides inflicted on the state by the super storm. **Jewel Samad/AFP/ Getty Images**

followed; the president also received high approval ratings for his handling of Hurricane Sandy, a massive storm that battered the East Coast and mid-Atlantic states just a week before the election. As the campaign continued in its final days, the margin between the candidates in the polls remained tight. On the eve of the election, the closely watched average of national polls compiled by the political news Web site RealClearPolitics. com showed Obama leading Romney 48.8 percent to 48.1 percent among likely voters.

CONCLUSION

On November 6, 2012, American voters headed to their polling places to determine—for the 57th time in U.S. history—who would be the country's president for the next four years. Despite the closeness of the race going into the election, President Obama emerged with a clear victory on election night, winning a sizable majority in the electoral college to secure a second term in the White House. The president claimed at least 303 electoral votes to challenger Mitt Romney's 206 and in the process swept virtually all of the so-called battleground states where the presidential race had been most hotly contested, including Ohio, Colorado, Virginia, Iowa, Wisconsin, and New Hampshire, among others. For his part, Romney was able to carry only two of the states that Obama had won in the 2008 election—Indiana and North Carolina. The final margin in the popular vote stood at more than 50 percent for Obama and Vice President Biden to around 48 percent for the Romney-Ryan ticket. In his late-night victory speech in Chicago, Obama thanked voters across the country and proclaimed, "Tonight, in this election, you, the American people, reminded us that while our road has been hard, while our journey has been long, we have picked ourselves up, we have fought our way back, and we know in our hearts that for the United States of America the best is yet to come."

As expected, exit polls conducted on election day showed that voters overwhelmingly cited the ailing economy as their top concern. At the same time, however, voters appeared to recognize that the economy was slowly improving and were willing to give the president more time to address the array of problems confronting the country. As Obama turned his attention toward the next four years, the question in the minds of many observers was just how productive he would be in his second term given that the government remained sharply divided. Although a record-breaking amount of money—an estimated $6 billion—was poured into the election, in the end the balance of power in Congress was relatively unchanged, as Republicans retained solid control of the House of Representatives and Democrats increased their majority slightly by two seats in the Senate.

Obama's calls for bipartisanship cooperation seemed more urgent than ever. As the election was unfolding, the country was drawing closer to what Federal Reserve Chairman Ben Bernanke had dubbed the "fiscal cliff," a series of economic measures mandated by law to either expire or be enforced at the turn of the new year. These included the expiration of tax cuts passed during the presidency of George W. Bush, temporary payroll tax cuts initiated by the Obama administration, and some tax breaks for businesses, along with the automatic application of across-the-board spending cuts to military and nonmilitary programs as required by the budget agreement of 2011. There was fear that, absent some compromise, those measures would result in another recession.

Aside from tackling the daunting economic and fiscal issues, another major goal for Obama's second term was to oversee the continued implementation of the Patient Protection and Affordable Care Act, the health care reform legislation put into place by his administration. Obama's reelection alone represented a major step toward ensuring the survival of the sweeping reforms, since Romney had promised to revoke the legislation if he were elected. The historic law would extend health care coverage to millions of previously uninsured Americans.

While Obama acknowledged in his victory speech the difficulties that lie ahead, he continued to stress his optimism for the future. His closing lines, in fact, were reminiscent of his stirring keynote address at the 2004 Democratic National Convention, which had first brought him to the attention of the country at large. "I believe we can seize this future together," said the newly reelected president, "because we are not as divided as our politics suggests. We're not as cynical as the pundits believe. We are greater than the sum of our individual ambitions, and we remain more than a collection of red states and blue states. We are and forever will be the United States of America."

Glossary

ascetic Harshly simple; austere.

bellwether A person, place, or thing that leads the way or points out a trend.

default Failure to carry out a contract, obligation, or duty.

deficit When a person, business, or government spends more money than is taken in.

delegate A person who acts as a representative for others at a convention or conference.

deploy To move, spread out, or place in position for some purpose (as with military troops to battle).

filibuster The use of delaying tactics (as long speeches) to put off or prevent action, especially in a legislative assembly. The record for a single uninterrupted speech in the U.S. Senate is more than 24 hours.

gridlock A situation resembling a highly congested traffic jam in which no forward movement is possible.

Gross Domestic Product (GDP) The government uses GDP as the best indicator of overall economic health because it represents the total market value of all goods and services during a given year. Unlike the better-known Gross National Product (GNP), GDP omits income from overseas investment.

magna cum laude Latin phrase meaning "with great distinction."

obstructionism Deliberate interference with business, especially in a legislative body.

partisan Strong devotion to a particular cause or group. A partisan person may be said to exhibit blind, prejudiced, and unreasoning allegiance.

polemic A controversial discussion or argument.

pundit One who gives opinions in an authoritative manner; a critic.

received Generally accepted.

stimulus package A group of actions by a government meant to encourage economic growth.

stump To go about making political speeches in support of a cause or candidacy.

up the ante Borrowed from the game of poker, an expression meaning to raise the stakes.

For More Information

American Historical Association (AHA)
400 A Street, SE
Washington, DC 20003
(202) 544-2422
Web site: http://www.historians.org
The AHA serves as a leader and advocate for professionals, researchers, and students in the field of history. The AHA also awards a number of fellowships and prizes, offering important resources and publications for anyone interested in the field.

Association for the Study of African American Life and History (ASALH)
Howard Center
2225 Georgia Avenue, NW
Suite 331
Washington, DC 20059
(202) 238-5910

Web site: http://www.asalh.org

The ASALH supports education, research, and scholarship on African American history and culture and preserves the legacies of African American pioneers in a variety of fields.

National Museum of American History (NMAH)

1400 Constitution Avenue NW

Washington, DC 20560

(202) 633-1000

Web site: http://americanhistory.si.edu

With more than three million artifacts of American history in its collection, many of which are on display, the NMAH is dedicated to promoting public interest in the events that have shaped the American nation. Its The American Presidency: A Glorious Burden exhibit profiles American presidents through collections of their personal belongings, campaign memorabilia, and many other items.

National Portrait Gallery

Eighth and F Streets, NW

Washington, DC 20001

(202) 633-8300

Web site: http://www.npg.si.edu

From activists to artists to celebrities to presidents, the National Portrait Gallery celebrates individuals who have had a significant impact on American culture. Shepard Fairey's iconic Hope (2008), a portrait of Barack Obama, is among its vast collection.

WEB SITES

Due to the changing nature of Internet links, Rosen Educational Services has developed an online list of Web sites related to the subject of this book. This site is updated regularly. Please use this link to access the list:

www.rosenlinks.com/pppl/baroba

Bibliography

Abramson, Jill. *Obama: The Historic Journey* (Callaway, 2009).

Corey, Shana, and Bernardin, James. *Barack Obama: Out of Many, One* (Random House, 2009).

Feinstein, Stephen. *Barack Obama* (Enslow, 2008).

Mendell, David. *Obama: From Promise to Power* (Amistad, 2007).

Mundy, Liza. *Michelle: A Biography* (Simon & Schuster, 2008).

Raatma, Lucia. *Michelle Obama* (Capstone Press, 2011).

Robinson, Tom. *Barack Obama: 44th U.S. President* (ABDO, 2009).

Schuman, Michael. *Barack Obama: "We Are One People,"* rev. and exp. ed. (Enslow, 2009).

Sutcliffe, Jane. *Barack Obama* (Lerner, 2010).

Wagner, Heather Lehr. *Barack Obama* (Chelsea House, 2008).

Wilson, John K. *Barack Obama: This Improbable Quest* (Paradigm, 2009).

Index